Sep+ 11/93

FOR CHRISTOPH

WITH LOVE FROM

Alison & Martin

D0119952

THE BIBLE
TELLS ME SO

Books in First Steps series

First Steps

The Bible Tells Me So

THE BIBLE TELLS ME SO

Paul J. Loth

Illustrated by
Daniel J. Hochstatter

THOMAS NELSON PUBLISHERS
Nashville

Published in Nashville, Tennessee, by Oliver-Nelson Books, a division of Thomas Nelson, Inc., Publishers, and distributed in Canada by Word Communications, Ltd., Richmond, British Columbia.

The Bible version used in this publication is the Contemporary English Version. Copyright © 1991, by the American Bible Society. Scripture noted NKJV is from THE NEW KING JAMES VERSION. Copyright © 1979, 1980, 1982, Thomas Nelson, Inc., Publishers.

Printed in the United States of America.

ISBN 0-8407-9232-8

1 2 3 4 5 6 7 — 98 97 96 95 94 93

Contents

About the Future

An Open Letter to Parents

One of the favorite times of the day with our children is our time of family devotions. It is during this time that we can talk about God and His Word. We can listen to our children talk about their concerns as well and can answer questions about the Lord. *The Bible Tells Me So* seeks to provide an opportunity to help our children understand the basic beliefs of our faith as presented in the Bible.

Quality time with our children is difficult to have in today's fast-paced world. That is why the family devotional time must include listening as well as talking.

Perhaps the greatest key to the success of family devotions is having a consistent time. Find a time that is free from distractions and scheduling conflicts. The length of time is not nearly so significant as its frequency and consistency.

The Bible Tells Me So is a unique family devotional. It is for families with young children desiring a family devotional time that includes time for talking about the Lord. Children have many questions about God. And the Bible has many answers. The family devotions in this book will not only provide instruction about what the Bible teaches about God but will also provide the framework for family discussions, questions, and further explanations.

This is done in four steps:

The Thinking Step If young children are to appreciate what the Bible says to them, they must identify its application to their lives right now. This time in your family devotions allows your family opportunity to explore your life today.

The Listening Step Beliefs in the Christian life must come from the Bible. This step presents the biblical teachings about our basic beliefs as Christians.

The Talking Step Talking together as a family is perhaps the most significant part of family devotions. This step provides questions to guide family discussions. It is at this time that the biblical teachings can be reinforced and applied to specific life situations and applications.

The Praying Step As the saying goes, "The family that prays together, stays together." Teaching our children to pray to their heavenly Father should be a special emphasis of every parent.

At the conclusion of each family devotional time is a Scripture verse which summarizes the teaching of the lesson. Many families will work with their children to memorize these verses. They will keep the focus of the lesson clearly upon God's Word.

May you and your children find these devotionals helpful in enlarging your understanding of our beliefs as members of the household of faith. And may they be used to draw your family closer together around His throne.

Paul J. Loth, Ed.D.

The Bible Is the Word of God

Exodus 19:10–25; 2 Timothy 3:10–17

The Thinking Step

Why do your brothers and sisters listen to your mother or father when they will not listen to you?

The Listening Step

When God spoke to Moses, the earth shook. Whenever God spoke, people listened. They listened to every word He said.

God's words are still important today. And God speaks to us, too. God speaks to us in the Bible. The Bible is God's Word. Paul wrote that the Bible was given by God. God told the writers what to write and they wrote it.

Many times in the Bible we read the words "God said." When a writer used those words, everyone listened. They wanted to hear the words of God.

When we read the Bible we can start with those words, too. "God said" is true of everything in the Bible. When we read the Bible we are reading the words of God.

The Talking Step

Name a time you have wanted to know what God thought about something. Did you find an answer in the Bible?

 **The Praying Step**

Sometimes I wish I could hear Your voice tell me something. But then I remember that I can read the Bible and know what You want to tell me.

> What God has said is not only alive and active! It is sharper than any double-edged sword. His word can cut through our spirits and souls and through our joints and marrow, until it discovers the desires and thoughts of our hearts.
>
> *—Hebrews 4:12*

11

The Bible Lasts Forever

Isaiah 40:1–8

 ## The Thinking Step

What is the oldest book you have ever seen?

Why would an old book be special?

 ## The Listening Step

Isaiah loved God. God thought Isaiah was special. He was God's messenger. He told people what God wanted them to know. God first told Isaiah. Then Isaiah told the people.

One day God said to Isaiah, "Cry out to the people!"

"What shall I tell the people?" Isaiah asked God.

"Tell them that flowers fade and grass dies, but God's Word lasts forever," God said.

The Bible was written a long time ago. Many people have tried to destroy the Bible. Others have tried to prove that the Bible is not true. But everything in the Bible has come true. Books have passed on. People have died. What the Bible says remains. The Bible really does last forever.

The Talking Step

Do you think your grandparents read the Bible?

Do you think your grandchildren will read the Bible?

Why does the Bible last forever?

 ## The Praying Step

Things change all the time: People move away or die, plants die, pets die, we all get older. Thank You that Your word never changes. Help me to study Your word and keep it in my heart.

> The grass withers, the flower fades, but the word of our God stands forever.
>
> —*Isaiah 40:8* NKJV

The Bible Is True

2 Timothy 2:15

The Thinking Step

Do you believe everything you read?
   Why? Why not?

The Listening Step

God always tells the truth. God told the people of Israel many things. He was right every time. God never lied. He was never wrong.

   The Bible is called the "Word of Truth." That is why. It is God's word and it is true. When we read the Bible we know we are reading the truth. We might not understand everything we read. But we know what we read is true.

   Paul was about to die. He wanted his young friend Timothy to know God better. He told Timothy to study the Bible. When we know the Bible, we know the truth. The Bible is truth.

The Talking Step

Have you ever argued with one of your friends about what is true and what is not true?

   Have you ever wondered what is the right way to believe?

✋ The Praying Step

I know the Bible is the truth and I should study it more often. Help me find time to read the Bible and memorize what it says. Thank You for Your word.

> All you say can be trusted. Your teachings are true and will last forever.
> —*Psalm 119:160*

Angels: God's Special Helpers

Luke 2:8–15, 24:1–8; Acts 1:6–11, 5:12–20

 ## The Thinking Step

Who is the most important person you know?
    Does that person have special helpers?
    Who are those helpers?
    What do the helpers do?

The Listening Step

Angels were special helpers for Jesus. They told the shepherds when Jesus was born. And they rolled away the stone after He came alive.

Then Jesus went back to heaven. The angels helped the disciples then. They told them what to do. The angels helped free Peter from jail.

Angels help God do a lot of things. Angels help us, too. They watch over our lives. They are special helpers of God.

 ## The Talking Step

How do angels help you?
    Thank God for having angels watch over you.

🖐 The Praying Step

Thank You for sending angels to watch over me. It makes me feel good to know they are around me, taking care of me and helping me.

> Angels are merely spirits sent to serve people who are going to be saved.
> —*Hebrews 1:14*

God Is Faithful

Matthew 8:18–27; 14:22–33; 28:16–20

The Thinking Step

Have you ever had friends not keep their promises? What happened?
How did you feel about your friends after they let you down?

The Listening Step

Jesus was talking to His friends. He was saying goodbye. He was going to heaven.

Jesus said He would always be with them. The disciples believed Him. They remembered a special time. They were in the middle of a bad storm. Jesus stood up in the boat. Then He looked out over the high waves. "Peace! Be still!" Jesus said. And the storm stopped.

The disciples thought about this. They believed Jesus.

He will always be with us, too. We can always believe Him. God keeps His promises. God is faithful.

The Talking Step

Why are you glad God is faithful?
How have you seen God's faithfulness in your life?
In the life of your parents? Your grandparents?

The Praying Step

When I am lonely, I feel better knowing that Jesus is always with me. I am glad that I can always believe what You promise. Thank You for always keeping Your word.

> God can be trusted, and he chose you to be partners with his Son, our Lord Jesus Christ.
>
> —*1 Corinthians 1:9*

God Is Holy

Exodus 3, 19; 1 Peter 1:16

The Thinking Step

What does it mean when something is pure—pure milk, pure butter, pure American?

The Listening Step

God is special. He is pure and holy. Moses learned that. One day Moses was walking through the fields. He saw a bush burning. But the bush kept burning on and on. It did not stop. "Moses!" a voice called to him from the bush. Moses knew he was speaking with the Lord.

Many years later Moses would climb to the top of a mountain to talk with God. The people of Israel could not touch the mountain. They had to watch from the ground below. The Lord was a holy God.

That is why Peter was afraid to be with Jesus. When Peter learned that Jesus was God's Son he said, "Lord, don't come near me! I am a sinner." But Jesus loved Peter. It was the sinners whom Jesus came to save. Later Peter would remind Christians to be holy because God is holy.

Someday we will be like God. We will be holy, too.

The Talking Step

Are you holy now?

What could you do to be more like our holy God?

✋ The Praying Step

Pure and *holy* are hard words to understand. But I guess a pure Christian would be one who was very much like You. That is what I want to be, Lord. Help me to be like You.

> I am the holy God, and you must be holy too.
>
> —*1 Peter 1:16*

God Is in Charge of Everything

Genesis 1; Mark 4:35–41

 ## The Thinking Step

Who is in charge?

At home? In your town? At school? At church?

Is there anyone who is in charge of everyone and everything?

The Listening Step

God made the world. He made everything in the earth. God wanted us to have a nice place to live. He wanted us to enjoy the earth.

One day Jesus and His disciples were taking a boat ride. It was very windy. Soon a storm came across the lake. The boat started to tip. The disciples were scared. They were trying as hard as they could to keep the boat from tipping over. But Jesus was asleep in the back of the boat. "Teacher, don't You care that we're about to drown?" they asked Jesus as they woke Him.

Jesus got up and walked to the edge of the boat. He held out His hands and told the storm to stop. Right away the waves stopped. The winds died down. The disciples were amazed. "Even the wind and waves obey Him," they said.

 ## The Talking Step

Name a time you remember seeing God in charge.

Name a time you were glad God was in charge.

🤲 The Praying Step

I am glad that You are in charge. I am glad to belong to the One who controls the winds and the waves.

God's Son was before all else, and by him everything is held together.
—*Colossians 1:17*

God Is Just

Romans 2:1–16

The Thinking Step

Have you ever said, "It's not fair!"? Why?

Whom do you know who always decides fairly?

Anyone ever say to you, "It's not fair"?

The Listening Step

It may seem that God is not paying attention. But He is. He sees what is going on. He remembers. A long time ago people were doing many wrong things. Paul told them that God would judge them for what they had done.

"God will judge fairly," Paul wrote. "Those who do the wrong thing will be punished. Those who do the right thing will be rewarded." Many people thought that God would give them special treatment. But Paul said no. God will judge everyone according to how they live their lives.

God is fair. He will judge each of us fairly.

The Talking Step

Are you glad God is fair in how He judges people? Why?

Name a time God judged someone fairly. Did He punish or reward that person?

🖐 The Praying Step

Things in our world do not always happen fairly. I get discouraged about that. Thank You for always being fair in what You do. That makes the unfairness around me easier to take.

> You see that justice is done.
>
> —*Psalm 7:11*

God Is Love

John 15:9–17; 1 John 3:11—4:21

The Thinking Step

How would you describe one of your friends in one word?
  What word would your friends use to describe you?
  That would need to be a very important word, wouldn't it?

The Listening Step

Jesus said that we must love one another. This would show that we belong to Him. That is what God is like—love.

John was a disciple whom Jesus loved very much. John remembered what Jesus said. John repeated it years later. He wrote it in a letter. "If you do not love one another you do not belong to God," John wrote. "God is love."

The one word that describes God is *love*. God loved us so much that He sent Jesus to die for us. He takes care of us. He does what is best for us every day. This is how God shows love.

The Talking Step

How do you know that God is love?
  What has God done for you this week to show you that He is love?

 **The Praying Step**

Some people are not easy to love. I want to let You love those people through me. I pray that people will know that I love You because of how I treat others.

> My dear friends, we must love each other. Love comes from God, and when we love each other, it shows that we have been given new life.
>
> —*1 John 4:7*

God Is Merciful

Matthew 18:21–35

The Thinking Step

When was the last time you did something wrong?
Did you get punished? Did you get what you deserved for what you did?
When have you done something wrong and not received what you deserved?

The Listening Step

It is a good thing God does not give us what we deserve. Jesus wanted people to know that. So Jesus told them this story.

A man owed a lot of money. He was not able to pay back all the money. So the man talked to the person to whom he owed the money. "I cannot pay you all the money I owe," the man said. "Please do not make me pay all this money." The man felt sorry for him. So he let him go without paying back all the money.

This is how God treats us. We deserve to be punished for all the things we do wrong. But God loves us. He lets us go. And He does not give us what we deserve. That is because God is merciful.

The Talking Step

What does it mean that God is merciful?
Why do you think God does not give us what we deserve?

28

![hand icon] **The Praying Step**

Thank You for not giving me what I really deserve. Help me to follow Your example in the way I treat my family and friends.

> You are truly merciful.
>
> —*Psalm 69:16*

God Is Our Father

Matthew 6:9–13

 The Thinking Step

What does a parent do?

Are parents always nice?

Do parents try to do things to help their children?

The Listening Step

The disciples wanted to learn to pray. They wanted Jesus to teach them. Jesus began His prayer in a special way. "Our Father," Jesus began. The disciples were afraid of God. God was powerful. He made the world. Now Jesus was telling them to call Him Father.

They did not understand. They knew Jesus was the Son of God. But how did that make Him *their* Father? They were special. Jesus lived inside of them. This made God their father, too.

We are special now. Because of Jesus, God accepts us as His children. And God is our Father. We have a special relationship with God. He is our Father.

The Talking Step

How should we act toward God as our Father?

How does God treat us as His children?

🖐 The Praying Step

A father should be obeyed and loved. A father takes care of his children and helps them with their problems. Thank You for being my loving, perfect Father.

> You will be my sons and my daughters, as surely as I am God, the all-powerful. I will be a Father to You.
>
> —*2 Corinthians 6:18*

God Is Strongest

Exodus 5–11; 1 Samuel 17

The Thinking Step

Who is the strongest person you know?
Who is the strongest person you have ever seen?
Could this person shake a mountain or defeat an army?

The Listening Step

Egypt was a strong nation. Their army was very big. It was one of the biggest in the world. Pharaoh was the king of Egypt. He thought he was the strongest man in the world. Moses went to talk to Pharaoh. He took his brother Aaron with him. They told him that God was stronger. They told Pharaoh he should do what God wanted. But Pharaoh would not listen. So God had to show that He was the strongest.

God did many things. He proved He was the strongest. Finally Pharaoh believed. He knew that God was the strongest. He did what God wanted. He let the people of Israel leave Egypt.

God is all-powerful. There is nothing God cannot do. God is the strongest.

The Talking Step

Why is it good to know that God can do anything?
Name a time you were glad God is all-powerful.

 **The Praying Step**

Knowing that You can do anything gives me courage to pray for hard things.
I know that You care about whatever matters to me. I know that You have
enough power to do something about it.

Nothing is impossible for God!

—*Luke 1:37*

God Is the Boss

Exodus 5—14

 The Thinking Step

Whom do you know who can do whatever they want?
Do you know someone who does not have a boss?

The Listening Step

Pharaoh in Egypt thought he did not have a boss. IIe thought he could do whatever he wanted. Moses told him that God wanted the people of Israel to leave. Pharaoh laughed. But he was wrong. God is the only one who can do whatever He wants. God does not have a boss. He is the boss.

But God had to prove that. Pharaoh did not know this. God let many bad things happen to Pharaoh. Finally the king learned that God is in charge. Everyone should obey Him.

Our God does whatever He likes. It is good to be on God's side. He will take care of us.

The Talking Step

Is it good that God is in charge of the world? Why? Why not?

 **The Praying Step**

You sure showed Pharaoh! I am glad You are in charge of the world. I am glad You are in charge of me, because I know You love me and will always do what is best for me.

> God has put all things under the power of Christ, and for the good of the church he has made him the head of everything.
>
> —*Ephesians 1:22*

God Is Three in One

Matthew 6:9–13, 28:19; Luke 3:21–22; 2 Corinthians 13:13

The Thinking Step

How many people do you have in your family?

How many families do your mom and dad and your brothers and sisters make? One? Or more?

The Listening Step

God is talked about many times in the Bible. God made the world. And the Spirit of God moved around the earth. Jesus, who is God's Son, came to earth as a person.

God's family has three members, the Father, the Son, and the Spirit. Each member of God's family is God even though there are three of them. Each of them is still God.

We have special jobs in our family. And the Father, Son, and Spirit have special jobs, too. God made us. Jesus died for us. And the Spirit helps us.

It is good that there are three members of God's family. We need all three of them.

The Talking Step

The next time you read the Bible, look for the three members of God's family.

Maybe you can find all three in the same verse.

How do all three members of God's family help us?

 **The Praying Step**

Being part of a family is a special feeling. Thank You that I am part of Your family. Thank You for the three members of Your family who do their special jobs to take care of me.

> I pray that the Lord Jesus Christ will bless you and be kind to you! May God bless you with his love, and may the Holy Spirit join all your hearts together.
>
> —*2 Corinthians 13:13*

God Knows Everything

Psalm 139; John 21:1–8

The Thinking Step

When was the last time you told someone, "You think you know everything!"?
Is there anyone who knows everything?

The Listening Step

Jesus knows everything. One day the disciples were fishing. They were not having any luck. Jesus told them where to fish. He said to try the other side of the boat. They did. They caught a lot of fish. They caught so many the boat began to sink! Jesus knows everything. He even knew where the fish were.

King David was happy that God knew everything. "You know where I am," David wrote. "You know what I am thinking. You even know every word I speak." David was sure God knew everything. He knew God would take care of him.

We can be sure. God knows everything.

The Talking Step

How does knowing everything help God take care of you?
Is there anything you are glad God knows about you and your life?
Is there anything you wish God did not know?
What will you do differently knowing that God knows everything?

 **The Praying Step**

I confess that there are things about me that I wish You did not know.
Forgive me for not always thinking and living the way I should.

> You have looked deep into my heart, LORD, and you know all about me.
>
> —*Psalm 139:1–2*

God Made Everything

Genesis 1

The Thinking Step

What do you like best about the world?
  Why do you think God made that?

The Listening Step

A long time ago there was nothing. There was no earth or trees. There was no land. There were no people! God made everything. He made it simply by wanting it to happen. The earth appeared. The trees, the land, and you and me just appeared, too.

Years later Paul wanted us to know what God had done. "Everything was created by him, everything in heaven and on earth," wrote Paul. God is the creator. He wanted us to have a beautiful earth in which to live. God wanted us to be happy. So He made the heavens and the earth for us.

This is one of the best ways to describe God. Explain that God is the creator. If God can create the entire world and universe simply by ordering it, He can take care of anything else He wants as well.

 ## The Talking Step

What is your favorite part of God's creation?
  Why is it important that God created the world?
  What does the creation of the world tell you about God?

 ## The Praying Step

Thank You for making me. I know that I am just what You wanted me to be.

> Everything was created by him, everything in heaven and on earth, everything seen and unseen, including all forces and powers, and all rulers and all authorities. All things were created by God's Son, and everything was made for him.
>
> —*Colossians 1:16*

God Never Changes

Exodus 12:1–36; Luke 2:1–32

The Thinking Step

How have you changed since last year?
>What changes have there been in your life since last year?
>What has changed in your family since last year?

The Listening Step

Everything changes. People change the way they look. Things in our life change. But God never changes.

The people of Israel were worried. They knew God loved them. And they knew He promised to save them. But they had waited for Jesus for a long time. Would God ever give them a Savior? They knew God took care of them. God saved them from Egypt. God protected them from the Red Sea. God helped David defeat Goliath. And God protected Israel from their enemies.

Soon an angel gave the good news. Jesus was born. God did keep His promise. He did send a Savior. Now the people of Israel knew for sure. God never changes.

The Talking Step

What is it that never changes about God?
>What does that mean to you?

42

The Praying Step

It seems like so many things around me are changing. Friends move away; people die; friends break promises. Thank You that You never change. I can always trust You.

> For I am the LORD, I do not change.
>
> —*Malachi 3:6* NKJV

The Lord Is the Only God

1 Kings 18

The Thinking Step

Do you have friends who believe in other religions?
Do they believe in other gods? Why?

The Listening Step

Elijah loved God. He wanted everyone to love God. But many of the people did not. They believed in another god, Baal. Elijah had to prove there is only one God.

He had an idea. "We will both make sacrifices to our Gods," Elijah said. "We will see which God starts a fire." The people thought that was a good idea.

The followers of Baal made a sacrifice to their god. They prayed to Baal. There was no response.

Now it was Elijah's turn. Elijah prepared the sacrifice. He even poured water on it. Then Elijah prayed to God. God sent a fire. The fire was so strong that it burned the whole thing up.

The people bowed down to God. They said they would follow only God from then on.

The Talking Step

Can there be other gods besides the Lord? Why? Why not?
Are you glad the Lord is the only true God? Why?

44

🖐 The Praying Step

You sure showed those followers of Baal. It's great to know that You are the most powerful; You are the true God. I'm glad I'm on Your side!

> You know the LORD is God!
>
> —*Psalm 100:3*

We Are Like God

Genesis 2:4–25

The Thinking Step

Has anyone ever told you that you look just like your mom or dad? Why? What makes members of your family similar?

The Listening Step

God was lonely. He made the world. He even made the animals. But still God was lonely. He needed someone to whom He could talk. So God made man and woman.

But God wanted man and woman to be different from the animals. "Let Us make man in Our image," God said. That would make man different from everything else God had made. Man and woman would have souls, an inside part. They could talk with God. And God could talk with them.

So God made man and woman. He made them special. They were like God.

The Talking Step

How do you feel knowing you were made like God? Does this help you talk to God better? How?

🤚 The Praying Step

Thank You that I can talk to You, anytime I want to. You are always listening, and You care what I am thinking about. Thank You that I am made like You, what could be better?

So God created man in His own image; in the image of God He created him; male and female He created them.

—*Genesis 1:27* NKJV

God Is Everywhere

Psalm 139

The Thinking Step

Have you ever thought that your mom and dad had "eyes in the back of their heads"? Why?

How would you feel or act if you knew someone was watching you all the time?

The Listening Step

David had a problem. He knew God was everywhere. David was a king of Israel. He knew that God knew everything about him. There was nowhere he could go to hide from God. God was everywhere!

David wrote a song about it. "Where could I go to escape from your Spirit? Or from your sight?" David wrote. David knew that God was there, no matter where he went. God was everywhere.

That meant that God knew everything David did. It also meant that God was there to help David when he needed help. David was glad that God was everywhere.

The Talking Step

How does knowing God is everywhere make you feel?

What does it make you want to do differently?

Explain how you will act and what you will do knowing that God is everywhere.

✋ The Praying Step

It is a little bit scary to know that You know everything I do and think. Help me to remember that every day. Then I can live my life so I won't be ashamed to have You see me all the time.

> Suppose I had wings like the dawning day and flew across the ocean. Even then your powerful arm would guide and protect me.
>
> —*Psalm 139:9–10*

God Has No Birthday

Genesis 1; John 1

The Thinking Step

When is your birthday?

Does your birthday change? Why not?

Do you know anyone who does not have a birthday?

The Listening Step

God made the world. God made the heavens and the earth. But God was here before He made the world. God was here when there was nothing else. God had no beginning. God was never born. God has no birthday.

And God will have no ending, either. He will never die. God has no beginning and God has no ending. Since God has no ending, we who belong to God will have no ending, either. God will one day bring us to heaven. We will be able to live with Him forever. And we will never die, either.

It is good to know that God had no beginning and will have no ending. Then we can live with Him forever.

The Talking Step

Are you glad God had no beginning and will have no end?

Why?

50

The Praying Step

It is hard to understand what it means to have no beginning and no ending. I am really glad that You will always be here for me, though. And that I can live forever with You.

> You have always been God—long before the birth of the mountains, even before you created the earth and the world.
>
> —*Psalm 90:2*

Jesus Holds Everything Together

Colossians 1:15–23

 ## The Thinking Step

Have you ever made a tower that won't stay up by itself?
What did you do? How did you keep it from falling over?

The Listening Step

God made the world. He put the stars in place. He made all the beautiful things on the earth. God also made you and me.

And God made sure everything stays the way He made it. Jesus keeps everything in order. Everything is held together in Him. God did not make the world and walk away. Jesus keeps things beautiful. He keeps the world special.

Our life can be like that. Jesus helps keep our life in order, too. Jesus is key to our life.

The Talking Step

What in your life centers on Jesus?
What could you do that would center on Jesus?

🤲 The Praying Step

Thank You for staying involved in our world and our lives. I want You to be in the center of my life. I love You.

God's Son was before all else, and by him everything is held together.
—*Colossians 1:17*

Jesus Is God

Mark 2:1–12

 The Thinking Step

Have you ever seen God?

What do you think He would look like?

The Listening Step

Jesus had just healed a man. The chief priests were not happy. Jesus had said something which made them angry. "Your sins are forgiven," Jesus told him. "Only God can forgive sins," the priests said.

That's right! That was what Jesus was trying to tell them. "I and the Father are One," Jesus said. Now they were really mad. But Jesus was only telling the truth. Jesus was God.

"When you have seen Me, you have seen the Father," Jesus told them.

The Talking Step

Are you glad Jesus is God?

Why?

What would you have done if you lived when Jesus did?

 **The Praying Step**

Please forgive my sins. I try not to sin, but sometimes it just happens. Help me to be stronger and to live my life so that others can see You by watching me.

> Christ is exactly like God, who cannot be seen. He is the firstborn son, superior to all creation.
>
> —*Colossians 1:15*

Jesus Is Head of the Church

Romans 12; 1 Corinthians 12; Ephesians 2:19–22, 4:11–16

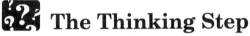 ## The Thinking Step

Have you ever tried to build a tower?
> What is the difference between a bad tower and a good tower?
> What is the most important piece of the tower?

The Listening Step

Paul liked to draw pictures. He did not draw with crayons. Paul drew pictures with words.

Paul drew a picture of the church. It was a picture of a person's body. He said it was a picture of the church. Everybody in the church is part of the body. Jesus is the most important part. He is the head. He tells the rest of the body what to do.

Paul drew another picture of the church. He drew a picture of a building. In this picture, Jesus is the cornerstone. This is the first piece of a building. It is the bottom piece of a tower. Everything is built on the cornerstone.

Jesus is the cornerstone. Everything begins with Him. Jesus is the head of the church.

 ## The Talking Step

What would your church be like if Jesus really were in charge?
> How does your church let Jesus be the head?
> What do you think Jesus wants to do as head of the church?

 **The Praying Step**

Help our church members to love each other. Help us to reach out to others and tell them about Your love. Thank You for my church.

> You are like a building with the apostles and prophets as the foundation and with Christ as the most important stone. And you are part of that building Christ has built as a place for God's own Spirit to live.
>
> —*Ephesians 2:20–21*

Jesus Is King

Isaiah 9:6–7; John 18:28–40; Philippians 2:6–11

The Thinking Step

What is a king?

What does a king do?

How do people feel about their king?

The Listening Step

King David was a famous king. He won many battles. Israel was strong while David was king. God told the people that someday another king would be born. He would rule forever.

The people looked forward to that. When Jesus came, they were surprised. They thought the king would take over the world. They thought He would rule like David. They thought He would win many battles. Jesus tried to explain, "My kingdom is not of this world."

Jesus is still king. Isaiah called Jesus "King of kings." Everyone in the world must obey Jesus. Someday all the world will know that Jesus is the king.

No other king is greater than Jesus.

The Talking Step

What does Jesus do as king?

How does Jesus help you as king?

What special privileges do you have as a child of the King of kings?

58

🖐 The Praying Step

Jesus, You are the King of kings. You are more powerful and wonderful than any king ever was. You are loving and kind. I praise You for who You are.

The glorious God is the only Ruler, the King of kings and Lord of lords.
—*1 Timothy 6:15*

Jesus Is Our Friend

John 15:9–17

The Thinking Step

Name your closest friends.
 Why are they such good friends?
 What makes a good friend?

The Listening Step

The disciples had been with Jesus for a long time. They loved Jesus very much. And Jesus loved them.

 "I don't call you servants any more," Jesus told the disciples. "I call you My friends. The greatest love a man has is to give his life for his friends."

 The disciples knew they would never have a better friend than Jesus. He was always with them. He always helped them. In the end, He died for them. Jesus was their best friend.

 Jesus is our best friend, too. He is always with us. And Jesus will take care of us. It is good to know we have a friend like Jesus.

The Talking Step

What could you do to be better friends with Jesus?
 How has Jesus been a good friend to you?

 **The Praying Step**

Thank You, Jesus, that You are always with me, in good times and bad. Since You are my friend, help me to make time to spend with You, talking to You and reading Your word.

And you are my friends, if you obey me.

—*John 15:14*

Jesus Is Our Lawyer

1 John 2:1

The Thinking Step

Have you ever been to a lawyer?
>Has your mom or dad?
>What does a lawyer do to help us?
>Why do people need lawyers?

The Listening Step

In the Old Testament, people were afraid of God. God met Moses on top of the mountain. Moses talked to God. He told the people of Israel what God said. The people could not talk to God.

If people sinned, they went to the priest. The priest gave a sacrifice to God. Only the priest could talk to God.

But Jesus changed that. Jesus is God's Son. Jesus can talk to God. Jesus lets us talk to God, too. When Jesus died, a special part of the temple opened. This was where the priests went to talk to God. Later, Peter wrote, "We are all priests."

Jesus talks to God for us now. We can talk to God, too. Because of Jesus, God lets us talk to Him. Aren't you glad Jesus is our friend?

The Talking Step

How do you think Jesus is like a lawyer?
>When was the last time you talked to God?
>Thank Jesus for making it possible for you to talk to God.

 ## The Praying Step

I am glad that I can talk to You anytime. I'm sorry that Jesus had to die so I could do this. Help me remember to talk to You more often.

> My children, I am writing this so that you will not sin. But if you do sin, Jesus Christ always does the right thing, and he will speak to the Father for us.
>
> —*1 John 2:1*

Jesus Is Our Savior

Matthew 26; John 18:1–11

The Thinking Step

Have you ever been in trouble and needed someone to save you?

What happened?

How did it feel to have someone save you?

The Listening Step

The disciples were scared. Jesus had told them that He would soon die. They did not want Him to die.

Then one night soldiers came to take Jesus away. Peter took his sword to protect Jesus. "Stop!" Jesus said. "This is why I came to earth. I came to die for the sins of the world."

Soon Jesus would die on the cross. We have all sinned. Each of us deserves to die for our sins. But Jesus died in our place. He saved us.

Jesus' mother, Mary, watched Jesus on the cross. She remembered what the angel said to Joseph before Jesus was born. "His name will be Jesus," the angel said. "He will save His people from their sins."

The Talking Step

Have you asked Jesus to save you from your sins?

Have you thanked Jesus for being your Savior?

Whom could you tell about Jesus being Savior of the world?

64

 **The Praying Step**

Thank You, Jesus, for being my Savior. You made a great sacrifice to do that. I have a special friend I want to tell about You. Please help me say the right words so my friend will understand.

> Name him Jesus, because he will save his people from their sins.
> *—Matthew 1:21*

Jesus Is the Lord

Philippians 1:1

The Thinking Step

Is there someone whom you always obey?
  Why?
  What would happen if you disobeyed that person?

The Listening Step

A long time ago, slaves helped people. Slaves did not get paid. They belonged to their owners. Slaves had to do what their owners told them to do. Slaves called their owners *lord* or *master*.

Jesus was called Lord and Master, too. In fact, Paul called himself a slave. He was a "slave of Jesus Christ." Paul belonged to Christ. He wanted to obey Him. Jesus was Lord over Paul's life.

If we love Jesus, He is our Lord as well. We belong to Jesus. We are to obey Him. We are to do whatever He says. Jesus is our Friend. He is our Savior. He is our Lord.

The Talking Step

Is Jesus Lord of your life?
  How do you know?
  Do you always do whatever Jesus says?
  How could you make Jesus Lord of your life, more than He is already?

The Praying Step

It is not easy to obey all the time. Even when it is You I am supposed to obey. Forgive me for not obeying, and give me strength to obey You all the time.

And to the glory of God the Father everyone will openly agree, "Jesus Christ is Lord!"

—Philippians 2:11

Jesus Is the Winner

John 19:16 — 20:18

The Thinking Step

When you play a game, do you try your best to win?
Do you think the best player always wins?

The Listening Step

Jesus had died. The Jewish leaders and priests had won. They had wanted to stop Jesus. Now they had stopped Him. At least they thought they had stopped Jesus.

One day Jesus' friends went to visit His grave. It was empty! They walked inside. There was an angel inside. "He is not here," the angel told them. "He is risen."

Jesus was alive! Jesus had won. Jesus died for us. And He became alive again. So we can live with Him forever in heaven.

When we have problems, we know Jesus can help us. He can overcome anything.

The Talking Step

What does it mean to be on the winning team?
What battle do you need Jesus to win for you?
Do you think He can win it? Why?

 **The Praying Step**

Those Jewish leaders must have been very surprised! Thank You that Jesus is alive. Thank You that Jesus is always helping me with my problems.

> But thank God for letting our Lord Jesus Christ give us the victory!
> —*1 Corinthians 15:57*

Jesus Will Always Be with Us

Matthew 28:16–20

The Thinking Step

What friend do you see most?

How often do you see this friend?

Do you think your friend will always be with you?

The Listening Step

The disciples were sad. They had been with Jesus for over three years. Jesus was very important to them. Now they knew Jesus was God's Son. He was the Savior of the world.

But Jesus was going back to heaven. The disciples were sad. How could they ever make it on their own?

But Jesus gave the disciples a special promise. He would still be with them! He would always be with them. He would be with them inside their hearts. Wherever they went, whatever they did, Jesus would be there. The disciples felt better now. Jesus would always be with them.

Jesus is always with us, too. He never leaves us.

The Talking Step

When have you been glad that Jesus is always with you?

70

🖐 The Praying Step

When someone I love goes away, I am very sad. I am glad that You never go away. I feel better knowing that You are always with me.

I will be with you always, even until the end of the world.

—*Matthew 28:20*

Jesus Is God's Son

Luke 3:7–22; John 17:6–28

The Thinking Step

Whom do you know who is a son?

How does his father feel about him?

Who has a better chance of getting favors from his father—you or his son?

The Listening Step

Jesus is special. He is God's Son. Jesus is special to God. Jesus was baptized in the Jordan River. When Jesus came out of the water, the heavens opened up. God said, "You are my beloved Son; in You I am well pleased."

Like any son, Jesus can ask God to do things. God will do them. Jesus prayed a prayer for us the night before He died. He asked God to keep us safe. He asked God to help us to always follow Him.

Those who believe in Jesus are able to ask God things. He will do them. We have a special relationship with God's Son. That means we are special to God as well. Jesus is special because He is the Son of God. If we accept Jesus, then God will accept us.

The Talking Step

Why is it special to you that Jesus is God's Son?

What can Jesus do for you by being the Son of God?

The Praying Step

Jesus, You are special because You loved me so much that You died for me.
I will be able to go to heaven because of what You did. Thank You, Jesus.
I love You.

You are the Messiah, the Son of the living God.
—*Matthew 16:16*

The Holy Spirit Assigns the Jobs

John 14:1–26; 1 Corinthians 12:1–11

The Thinking Step

What do you do well?

What abilities do your friends have?

The Listening Step

Jesus told the disciples they would do special things. They would tell people about Him.

Many people saw Jesus do miracles. He made the blind see. He healed the sick. He even brought the dead back to life. "You will even do more than I do," Jesus said. "You will have the Holy Spirit to help you."

The church is a special place. People in the church can do special things. The Holy Spirit helps them. But everyone does not do the same thing. Some people have special wisdom. Some people have special knowledge. Others are good at teaching. Everyone has a job to do. And when they do their job, the church is a special place. It is the Holy Spirit who gives the jobs to them.

The Talking Step

What special jobs has the Holy Spirit given to some of the people you know?

What special jobs has He given to you?

The Praying Step

It is hard to think that You might give me a job, since I am so young. Thank You for reminding me that I can do things for You. Show me exactly what You want me to do.

Each of you has been blessed with one of God's many wonderful gifts to be used in the service of others. So use your gift well.

—1 Peter 4:10

The Holy Spirit Guides Us

John 14:15–18, 16:5–15

The Thinking Step

Do you ever know what is the right thing to do?

How do you decide what is right?

Have you ever received the wrong guidance?

The Listening Step

The disciples always knew the right thing to do. If they had a question, they asked Jesus. He told them what to do. But now the disciples were worried. Jesus was leaving. If they had a question, whom could they ask?

"It is better for you that I leave," Jesus had told them. "Then the Holy Spirit can come. He will be your guide." Now the disciples felt better. The Holy Spirit would be part of them. He would be on the inside. He would guide them. He would help them make the right decisions.

Later the apostle Paul explained this. "Let the peace of Christ rule in your hearts," Paul wrote. That's how the Holy Spirit guides us. When we feel peace in our hearts, then we know we are obeying God.

The Talking Step

Have you ever had the Holy Spirit tell you what to do?

How did you know?

How can you help the Holy Spirit guide you?

The Praying Step

Thank You for the Holy Spirit. Help me remember to ask for help with decisions. Help me remember to see if I feel peace about decisions I make. Then I will know I am doing what You want.

> So let the peace that comes from Christ control your thoughts. And be grateful.
>
> —*Colossians 3:15*

The Holy Spirit Helped
Write the Bible

2 Timothy 3:16; 2 Peter 1:16–21

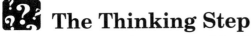 ## The Thinking Step

Have you ever written something?

Did someone tell you what to write?

Have you ever helped someone else write something?

The Listening Step

Many people wrote the Bible. Moses wrote part. David wrote some of the Psalms. Paul wrote much of the New Testament. There were many other writers, too. But the real writer of the Bible is the Holy Spirit.

Peter said the Bible is "God-breathed." God told the Holy Spirit what to say. The Holy Spirit told the writers of the Bible. Then they wrote what the Holy Spirit told them.

That is why the Bible is God's words. When we read the Bible, we are reading the words of God. That's what makes the Bible a special book.

 ## The Talking Step

How much of the Bible have you read?

Why should it be a special book?

How should reading the Bible help you?

78

 The Praying Step

Reading the Bible is the way that I can talk to You. I can learn what You think about just about anything, just by reading it. Thank You for giving us the Bible.

> The prophets did not think these things up on their own, but they were guided by the Spirit of God.
>
> —2 Peter 1:21

The Holy Spirit Helps People Believe in Jesus

John 16:7–15

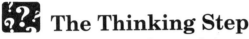 The Thinking Step

When have you tried to explain something to someone but had trouble? What did you do?

The Listening Step

Jesus told many people about God. The disciples saw this. They wanted to tell people, too. But many people did not listen to them. They did not want to hear about God. They did not know what to do.

Jesus said He would send help. He sent the Holy Spirit. The Holy Spirit tells people what they do wrong. He lets people know they need Jesus. He also tells them they will be punished.

People may not listen to us. The Holy Spirit will help us, too.

The Talking Step

Do you have a friend who does not think God will punish him? Have you asked God to convince your friend to trust in Jesus? Pray for your friend tonight.

 **The Praying Step**

I do have a friend who does not believe in Jesus. Please let the Holy Spirit tell my friend what he does wrong. Let my friend know that he needs Jesus.

> The Spirit will come and show the people of this world the truth about sin and God's justice and the judgment.
>
> —*John 16:8*

The Holy Spirit Helps Us Understand the Bible

John 14:15–26, 16:12–15

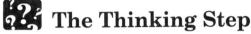 ## The Thinking Step

Do you understand everything you read?

What do you do if you do not understand something you read?

 ## The Listening Step

God knows everything. He knows much more than we do. That is why some of the Bible may be hard for us.

Jesus knew that. He knew we would not understand everything. That is why He sent the Holy Spirit. The Holy Spirit helped the disciples. He helped them understand what Jesus had said.

Jesus knew we needed help. He knew we did not understand all of the Bible. He sent the Holy Spirit to help us, too. The Holy Spirit helped write the Bible. He told the writers what to write. The Holy Spirit helps us, too. He helps us understand the Bible.

The Talking Step

Think of something in the Bible that you do not understand.

Ask the Holy Spirit to help you understand it.

✋ The Praying Step

It is good to know that I am not the only one who does not understand everything in the Bible. Thank You for giving me the Holy Spirit to help me understand.

> The Spirit shows what is true and will come and guide you into the full truth.
>
> —*John 16:13*

The Holy Spirit Helps Us Pray

Romans 8:18–30

The Thinking Step

When have you had trouble getting your friends to understand what you're saying?

The Listening Step

Different things concern us. What worries your friends may not worry you. And what worries you may not worry your friends. But God is concerned about each of us.

Sometimes it is hard to explain how we feel. We may understand how we feel. We may not be able to explain it. That is why God gave us the Holy Spirit. The Holy Spirit is inside each of us. He knows how we feel. We don't have to explain it.

When we pray, the Holy Spirit tells God how we feel. He can explain it better. He can help us pray.

The Talking Step

What would you like the Holy Spirit to help you pray for today?

Ask the Holy Spirit to help you pray.

The Praying Step

I don't always know what to pray for, or how to pray about some things. Thank You for the help I can get from the Holy Spirit.

> In certain ways we are weak, but the Spirit is here to help us. For example, when we don't know what to pray for, the Spirit prays for us in ways that cannot be put into words.
>
> —*Romans 8:26*

The Holy Spirit Teaches Us About God

John 16:12–15

 ## The Thinking Step

Who taught you about God?

How do you learn new things about God?

 ## The Listening Step

Jesus was leaving. His friends were not sure where to turn. They had always had Jesus. He had always been there to help.

Jesus was sending a helper to teach them. His friends did not know who it would be. They did not know whom Jesus was talking about. Later they found out.

The Holy Spirit came. He was their helper. "He will tell you what you need to know," Jesus said. Every Christian has the Holy Spirit. He lives inside us. The Holy Spirit teaches us about God.

 ## The Talking Step

How has the Holy Spirit taught you about God?

What has the Holy Spirit taught you about God?

🤚 The Praying Step

Thank You for the Holy Spirit. I am glad He will help me learn about God. I am glad that He is always with me.

> The Spirit will bring glory to me by taking my message and telling it to you.
>
> —*John 16:14*

Every Believer Has the Holy Spirit

John 14—16

The Thinking Step

Have your mom and dad ever gone on a trip by themselves?
Did they leave someone else to take care of you?
What was that person supposed to do?

The Listening Step

Jesus' disciples were sad. Jesus had told them that He would be leaving them soon. Jesus said it was a good thing for them that He was leaving. God would send Someone to comfort and take care of them. He would also take care of all those who believe in Jesus.

This person we call the Holy Spirit. Jesus called Him the Comforter. He lives inside us. He tells us what to do. He is like a close friend who is with us all the time. When Jesus was on earth, everyone wanted to be with Him. But Jesus could not be with everyone at once.

The Holy Spirit can. Each of us has the Holy Spirit. When we ask God what to do, the Holy Spirit will tell us. It is good that Jesus went away to heaven. Then we can have the Holy Spirit with us. He can be our special friend.

The Talking Step

Can you remember a time when the Holy Spirit helped you?
Why is it good that each of us has the Holy Spirit with us?

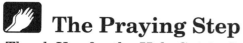 **The Praying Step**

Thank You for the Holy Spirit. I am glad that I have Him with me all the time. I am glad that He helps me everyday.

> Turn back to God! Be baptized in the name of Jesus Christ, so that your sins will be forgiven. Then you will be given the Holy Spirit.
>
> —*Acts 2:38*

Satan Is Captain of the Other Team

Matthew 4:1–11; Ephesians 6:10–20

The Thinking Step

Do you know someone who scares you?
What do you do when you see this person coming?

The Listening Step

Jesus is God's Son. God loves Jesus very much. Jesus has the power of God.

Jesus went into the desert. Satan tried to get Jesus to disobey God. Satan tried to trick Jesus. Satan wanted Jesus to obey him. Satan tried very hard. But Jesus did not fall for any of the tricks.

Satan is very strong. Many people fall for his tricks. Satan tricked Eve. He got her to disobey God in the Garden of Eden. Only Jesus is stronger than Satan.

Satan still tries to get people to do wrong things. But God is stronger than Satan. God will help us fight against Satan. All we need to do is ask Him.

The Talking Step

Has Satan tried to get you to do wrong things?
What did you do?
The next time Satan tries to get you to disobey God, ask God to help you.

 **The Praying Step**

Since Jesus was tempted by Satan, He understands when I am tempted. I don't want Satan to win in my life. Help me fight against temptation.

> Put on all the armor that God gives, so you can defend yourself against the devil's tricks.
>
> —*Ephesians 6:11*

Sin Is Disobeying God

Genesis 2:4—3:7; Exodus 20; Romans 3:9–31

The Thinking Step

Do you ever disobey your parents?

What happens?

How do you think God feels when you disobey Him?

The Listening Step

God made a beautiful world for Adam and Eve. God wanted everything perfect for them. He told Adam and Eve not to eat from a certain tree. They could not resist. They ate from the special tree. They disobeyed God. That made God very sad. That was the first sin. That is when sin came into the world.

Later God gave Moses the Ten Commandments. These were the laws that God expected the people to follow. But time after time they did not obey God. The Bible calls this *sin*. Everyone has sinned. None of us can live a perfect life.

God wants us to obey Him. We call it sin when we do not obey God. That is why we need to ask God to forgive us. And He does!

The Talking Step

When was the last time you disobeyed God?

Have you asked God to forgive you?

✋ The Praying Step

I am sorry for disobeying You. Please forgive me. Help me to obey You and show more love to my family and friends.

All of us have sinned and fallen short of God's glory.

—*Romans 3:23*

The Bad Forces in the World

Matthew 4:1–11; Ephesians 2:1–8, 6:10–20

 ## The Thinking Step

Have you ever tried to play a game and someone older than you keeps stopping the game?

Were you still able to play the game?

How did he or she stop you from playing the game?

The Listening Step

Satan did not like Jesus coming to the earth as a little baby. Jesus was telling people about God. Jesus told people to obey God and stop doing bad things.

But Satan wanted people to do bad things. He did not want people to obey God. Satan did not want people to believe in Jesus, either. That is why Satan tempted Jesus. He did not want Jesus to do what God wanted Him to do.

Satan is still in charge of this world. When we try to obey God, Satan tries to stop us. But we are not fighting alone. God will fight with us. He will defeat Satan. All we need to do is ask Him.

The Talking Step

What is happening today that shows Satan is in charge of the world?

Ask God to help you not let Satan control your life.

 **The Praying Step**

Thank You that I do not have to fight Satan alone. Thank You that You will help me. Please help me remember that You are always there for me.

> Be on your guard and stay awake. Your enemy, the devil, is like a roaring lion, sneaking around to find someone to attack.
>
> —*1 Peter 5:8*

The Battle Inside

Romans 7:13–25

The Thinking Step

Have you ever tried to be good *all* the time?

How did you do?

Why do you think it is so hard to always do the right thing?

The Listening Step

The apostle Paul had a problem. He always tried to be good. Paul went to a school that taught him the Bible. He even had one of the best private teachers. But he still had trouble being good.

Later in his life he wrote to the Christians in Rome about his problem. "I want to do the right thing, but I do the wrong thing. And I do what I do not want to do." Paul was upset. "There is something in me that makes me do the wrong thing," he writes to the Romans.

That is called a sin nature. It makes us do the wrong thing even if we want to do the right thing. But Paul gave his friends in Rome good news, too. Jesus helps us do the right thing. He helps us to obey God as we want.

The Talking Step

When was the last time you tried to do the right thing but did the wrong thing instead?

Ask God to help you obey Him better.

 ## The Praying Step

I know just how Paul felt. Sometimes I get discouraged that I can't do the right thing all the time. Please help me to trust You, and to use Your strength to be good, not my own strength.

> I know that my selfish desires won't let me do anything that is good. Even when I want to do right, I cannot.
>
> —*Romans 7:18*

The Punishment for Sin

Genesis 19; Matthew 4:1–11; Romans 3:9–31

The Thinking Step

Have you ever done anything wrong? What happened?

Were you punished?

Have you known someone who did wrong and was not punished?

The Listening Step

Jesus was perfect. He never did anything wrong. And He never sinned. He was tempted to do wrong. But Jesus still did not sin.

God hates sin. God will not allow sin to continue. Sin must be punished. When the people of Israel obeyed God, things went well. The people were punished when they sinned.

Sin is not obeying God. Paul wrote about sin. "Everyone sins," Paul wrote. "And the result of sin is death." God will punish sin. But God also sent Jesus to help us. Jesus died instead of us. When we believe in Jesus, we do not have to die for our sins. God loves us. He sent Jesus to die in our place.

The Talking Step

Do you think the punishment for sin is too hard?

Why does God not allow sin to go unpunished?

 **The Praying Step**

Thank You for making a way for us to be forgiven for our sins. I praise You for thinking of everything, and for giving so much. I love You.

> Sin pays off with death. But God's gift is eternal life given by Jesus Christ our Lord.
>
> —*Romans 6:23*

Wanting to Do the Wrong Thing

Romans 3:9–20, 7:15–25; Psalm 53

The Thinking Step

When your teacher or parents leave, what happens?

Does everyone do what is right or what is wrong?

If given a choice, will your friends try to do the right thing?

The Listening Step

The apostle Paul didn't understand why he acted this way. He knew what was right. He even *tried* to do what was right. But he couldn't. He still did what was wrong.

Paul probably thought about King David. God called David "a man after His own heart." But even David had trouble doing the right thing.

Maybe David was thinking about himself when he wrote, "They are corrupt, they have done abominable works. There is none who does good." People know how to do the wrong thing, David thought.

"Who can save me from this?" the apostle Paul asked. He knew the answer, too.

"Thank God," Paul said, "Jesus Christ will rescue me." Jesus helps us do the right thing.

The Talking Step

Ask Jesus to help you want to do the right thing.

Ask Jesus to help you obey Him.

 **The Praying Step**

Jesus, I want to obey You. Help me want to do the right thing, even when it is the hard thing to do. Give me Your strength to do the right thing.

But all of them are crooked and corrupt. Not one of them does right.

—*Psalm 53:3*

Jesus Helps Us Stop Sinning

Romans 7:13–25

 ## The Thinking Step

Have you ever felt that you can't stop doing the wrong thing?

Has there ever been a time in which you needed help being good?

The Listening Step

It can be hard to do the right thing. Disobeying is sometimes easier than obeying.

Jesus came to earth to die for our sins. We deserved to be punished. But Jesus was punished instead of us. Jesus saved us from being punished for our sins. Jesus also makes it easier for us to obey God.

Paul called himself "the chief of sinners." He wanted to do the right thing but he couldn't. The harder he tried to obey God, the more he disobeyed. What could Paul do? Paul wrote letters to his friends about his problem. "Jesus gives me the victory," Paul wrote. When we become Christians, Jesus changes our lives. We do not want to do bad things. Now we want to obey Jesus. We want to make Him happy.

Jesus will help us do the right thing. He changes us from the inside. Now we want to obey Him all the time.

 ## The Talking Step

Have you asked Jesus to help you obey Him?

How has Jesus helped you do the right thing?

The Praying Step

I want to do right things, but sometimes it is so hard. I start doing wrong things before I even realize it. Please give me strength to stop doing wrong things, help me to obey You.

Who will rescue me from this body that is doomed to die? Thank God! Jesus Christ will rescue me.

—*Romans 7:24–25*

Everyone Sins

Romans 1:18–32; Hebrews 4:15

The Thinking Step

Do you know anyone who is perfect?

Do your friends always do what their parents and teachers tell them?

The Listening Step

Jesus was the only One who lived a perfect life. Jesus never sinned. He never did anything wrong. When we want to know how to live our lives, we can look at the life of Jesus. He's the perfect example. His life is the life to follow.

Some of our friends live better lives than others. Some of our friends do many things wrong. Some of our friends do a few things wrong. But everyone does something wrong. Paul wrote that *all* have sinned. Everyone has done wrong things. Everyone has disobeyed God. No one has lived a life that is as perfect as Jesus' life. That's why we need God's help. We are not able to please God by ourselves. That's why Jesus came to earth. Everyone has fallen short of what God expects of us. Only Jesus can save us from our sins. He is perfect.

The Talking Step

What does it mean to you that Jesus saved you from your sins?

Did He have to do that?

What would have happened if He had not done that?

 **The Praying Step**

I am glad to have an example to follow. Knowing how Jesus lived on earth helps me know the right things to do. Thank You Jesus, for coming to earth.

All of us have sinned and fallen short of God's glory.
—*Romans 3:23*

Baptism: A Sign of Things Changed

Matthew 3; Romans 6:3–5

🔣 The Thinking Step

Have you ever gone anywhere and noticed that it was changed?
How did you know it was different?

👂 The Listening Step

John the Baptist lived in the desert. John told people to stop sinning. He told them Jesus was coming. He said they should ask God to forgive them.

Many people obeyed. They asked God to forgive them. Then they were baptized by John. They walked out into the water. John let them go under the water. Then he helped them out. This was a sign. It let people know they were following God. Even Jesus wanted John to baptize Him. Jesus wanted to give us an example to follow.

Many people believed in Jesus. They were baptized. Their faith in Jesus saved them. Baptism was a sign. It showed everyone that they were going to live for Christ.

🗣 The Talking Step

Have you seen someone get baptized? What happened?
Have you been baptized?

🤲 The Praying Step

Thank You for the examples Jesus gave us. Thank You that I can be saved. Thank You for signs like baptism that show others that I want to live for Jesus.

> Be baptized in the name of Jesus Christ, so that your sins will be forgiven.
>
> *—Acts 2:38*

Faith Is Believing

John 20:11–31

The Thinking Step

Have you ever had to have faith in something that was hard to believe?
    What was it?
    Why was it hard to believe?

The Listening Step

The disciples were happy. Jesus was alive! Thomas did not think it was true. He was sure Jesus was dead. He had to see Jesus with his own eyes. That is why he is called doubting Thomas.

One day Thomas did see Jesus. Jesus was alive! Thomas looked at Jesus. He touched Him. He finally believed. "You believe in Me because you see Me,"

Jesus said. "But others believe when they have not seen Me." That is faith. The other disciples had faith. They believed in Jesus even though they did not see Him. When we believe in Jesus we have faith. We do not see Him but we know He is real. Jesus likes that. He wants us to believe in Him.

The Talking Step

What would it be like to have faith in Jesus all the time?
    Why do we need to have faith to make Jesus happy?
    Do you have faith? When should you have had more faith?

🤲 The Praying Step

Sometimes it is hard to have faith. Especially when I don't see answers to my prayers right away. Thank You for being patient with me when I don't have as much faith as I should.

Faith makes us sure of what we hope for and gives us proof of what we cannot see.

—Hebrews 11:1

God Guarantees It

Ephesians 1:3–23

The Thinking Step

When was the last time someone broke a promise to you?

Has someone ever given you something to prove they would keep their promise?

The Listening Step

Jesus will save us from our sins. He promised this to us. If we ask Jesus into our heart we can claim this promise. We also become part of God's family. And Jesus will come and get us someday. We will be with Him in heaven forever.

But how do we know this will happen? How do we know God will keep His promise to us? God guarantees it. He sent the Holy Spirit to live in our hearts. So we know that we are part of God's family. And that He will come and bring us to heaven.

God made His home inside us. So we know we are part of His family.

The Talking Step

Do you ever wonder if you will go to heaven?

The next time you wonder that, think of the little voice inside of you. That is the Holy Spirit making His home in your heart.

The Praying Step

I'm glad that You always keep Your promises. I can believe that You will forgive my sins, if I confess them, and that I will live in heaven with You. Thank You that I can trust You.

The Spirit also makes us sure that we will be given what God has stored up for his people. Then we will be set free, and God will be honored and praised.

—*Ephesians 1:14*

God Isn't Mad Anymore

John 2:13–22; Romans 1:18–23

⁉️ The Thinking Step

Has your mom or dad ever been mad at you? Why?
What did you do to stop them from being mad?
Did it work?

👂 The Listening Step

One day Jesus visited the city. He went into the temple. He was going to worship God. What He saw made Him very angry. Men had set up tables in the temple. They were selling things. There were even animals in the temple! All of this made Jesus angry.

God gets angry, too. He gets angry at sin. In the old times people made sacrifices to God. Then God would not be angry with them.

God is angry when we sin. But Jesus helped us. He died for our sins. He became our sacrifice. Now God is not mad anymore.

🗣️ The Talking Step

Is God still angry at some people? Why?
Would you want God mad at you? Why? Why not?
Why is it good that God is not angry with us?

 ## The Praying Step

I really would not want You to be mad at me, God. Thank You, Jesus, for dying for my sins, so that God would not be angry anymore. That was a wonderful thing to do.

Christ is the sacrifice that takes away our sins and the sins of all the world's people.

—1 John 2:2

Jesus Makes Us Children of God

Galatians 4:1–11

The Thinking Step

Whose child are you?

What does that mean?

Do you get special privileges by being in your family that your friends do not get?

The Listening Step

Paul cared for the Galatians very much. Paul had told them about Jesus. He even helped them start their church. But Paul was worried about them. Jesus had done a lot for these people. Paul wanted them to know this.

"You are not a slave any more," Paul wrote to them. "You are now a child of God. And as a child of God, you receive part of God's kingdom." Jesus brought us into His family. It is the family of God. We are one of His children now. God is our father. And we will help run His kingdom.

We should be glad we are part of God's family!

The Talking Step

Are you one of God's children? Why?

What does that mean to you?

Whom do you know who is a brother or sister in God's family?

Is your mom or dad?

🤚 The Praying Step

Thank You for making me part of Your family. Thank You for loving me so much that You would die for me. Being part of Your family gives me a great inheritance.

Think how much the Father loves us. He loves us so much that he lets us be called his children, as we truly are.

—*1 John 3:1*

Jesus Paid the Penalty for Our Sin

John 1:19–34

 **The Thinking Step**

When was the last time you were punished for doing something wrong?

Has one of your friends ever offered to be punished for something you did? When?

The Listening Step

God wants everyone to obey Him. He does not like sin. God must punish sin. In old times people gave an animal to God. God accepted the animal. This was payment for the sin.

Later Jesus died on the cross. Jesus was special. He took away the sins of the world. Jesus was the payment. God accepted Jesus as payment for our sins.

Jesus died on the cross. He paid for our sin. Now we do not have to die. Jesus died in our place.

The Talking Step

Have you ever been punished for something someone else did?

Why do you think Jesus paid the penalty for us?

What does Jesus want us to do?

![hand icon] The Praying Step

I don't like to be punished, especially if I have not done anything wrong. You must really love me since You took my punishment. Thank You for that love.

Christ never sinned! But God treated him as a sinner, so that Christ could make us acceptable to God.

—*2 Corinthians 5:21*

Saved By Faith in Christ

Luke 23:26–49

The Thinking Step

Has anyone ever saved you? When? What happened?
What did you have to do to be saved?

The Listening Step

Jesus was dying on the cross. People were making fun of Him. The Roman soldiers were teasing Him.

Two robbers were dying, too. They were on crosses with Jesus. One robber made fun of Jesus. But the other robber believed in Jesus. "Remember me in Your kingdom," he said to Jesus. Jesus did more than that. "Today you will be with Me in heaven," Jesus said.

Maybe the man had heard Jesus talking earlier. "The only way to heaven is through Me," Jesus had said. Later John wrote, "Whoever believes in the Son of God has everlasting life."

The robber knew that Jesus was dying for him on the cross. All he had to do was believe. Jesus would be his Savior.

The Talking Step

Have you told Jesus that you love Him?
Have you accepted Jesus' death for you on the cross?
Have you asked Jesus to come into your heart and save you?

✋ The Praying Step

Thank You Jesus, for coming into my heart. I am so glad that I will live in heaven with You forever. I love You.

Yet some people accepted him and put their faith in him. So he gave them the right to be the children of God.

—John 1:12

We Are Chosen

John 15:1–17

 ## The Thinking Step

Do you have a pet in your house?
  What kind of pet is it?
  How did you decide what pet to have?

The Listening Step

The disciples were special to Jesus. And Jesus was special to them. They talked together often. This time Jesus told them things they did not understand.

"You are no longer slaves," Jesus said. "You are My friends." This was good. It was special to be a friend of Jesus. They were glad that Jesus was their friend. But Jesus had more to tell them.

"You did not choose Me," Jesus said. "I chose you even before the world was made."

A long time ago God knew we would be born. He chose us to be His children! We are special children of God. God wanted us. We were chosen by Him.

The Talking Step

How do you feel knowing that you were chosen by God?
  Thank God for choosing you.
  Ask Him to help you be a good child.

 The Praying Step

It makes me feel very special to know You chose me, and You made me to be just who I am. Thank You for loving me so much. I love You, too.

Before the world was created, God had Christ choose us to live with him and to be his holy and innocent and loving people.

—*Ephesians 1:4*

We Are Safe with Jesus Forever

John 10:22–30; Romans 8:31–39

 ## The Thinking Step

How long will you be a member of your family?

Will you no longer be a member of your family if you do bad things? Why?

The Listening Step

A shepherd has an important job. A shepherd takes care of the sheep. He watches the sheep. It is the shepherd's job to be sure that no one hurts the sheep. The shepherd keeps the sheep safe.

Jesus is like a shepherd to us. He makes sure we are kept safe. Jesus protects us. No one can take us away because Jesus is watching.

When we ask Jesus to be our Savior, we are safe. Jesus will always be our Savior. Nothing can change that.

The Talking Step

Thank Jesus for keeping you safe in His arms.

Thank Him for watching over you and keeping you one of His children.

 **The Praying Step**

Thank You, Jesus. Thank You that nothing happens to me that You don't know about.

> I am sure that nothing can separate us from God's love—not life or death, not angels or Spirits, not the present or the future, and not powers above or powers below. Nothing in all creation can separate us from God's love for us in Christ Jesus our Lord!
>
> —*Romans 8:38–39*

There Is Only One Way to Heaven

John 14:1–11

The Thinking Step

If you asked your friends how to get to heaven, what would they say?

What would your mom and dad say?

What do you say?

The Listening Step

The disciples were confused. Jesus was leaving. They did not know where He was going. They did not understand that Jesus was going to die.

"You know the way where I am going," Jesus told them. But that did not help. "We do not know where You are going," they said. "How can we know the way?"

"I am the Way," Jesus explained to them. "No one comes to the Father except through Me." Now the disciples were beginning to understand. Jesus was going to heaven. And if they believed in Him, they would go to heaven, too.

The Talking Step

How do people get to heaven?

Are you trusting in Jesus to go to heaven?

Have you asked Jesus to be your Savior?

The Praying Step

I want to know that I can live in heaven with You someday, Jesus. Please forgive my sins and come into my heart. Live in me, then I can know that I will live in heaven with You.

> I am the Way, the Truth, and the Life. Without me, no one can go to the Father.
>
> —*John 14:6*

We Are Saints

Romans 1:7; Ephesians 1:1

The Thinking Steps

Have you ever heard someone say, "You're no saint"?

What do you think they meant?

Do you know you really *are* a saint?

The Listening Step

Paul told a lot of people about Jesus. Many of these people became Christians. Then Paul helped start new churches. The new Christians were part of these churches. Later Paul wrote letters to the churches. These letters make up much of the Bible.

Paul wrote interesting letters to these churches. He did not start the letters "Dear. . . ." Paul started his letters "To the saints. . . ." Saint means someone who has done nothing wrong.

We can be saints. We must ask Jesus into our heart. Then He forgives us. It is like we have done no wrong. So we are all saints. When God looks at us, He sees people who are without sin.

The Talking Step

Would your friends think you're a "saint"? Why? Why not?

How could you better live like a saint?

126

 **The Praying Step**

I'm glad that You see me as if I have done nothing wrong, because of Jesus' sacrifice. Help me to live so that my friends will see I am different from others. Help me to tell them why I am different.

You Gentiles are no longer strangers and foreigners. You are citizens with everyone else who belongs to the family of God.

—*Ephesians 2:19*

Jesus Started the Church

Matthew 16:13–20

The Thinking Step

Did you ever help to start a club or a church?

Do you know someone who has helped start a company, church, or club?

Does that person decide what kind of group it will be? Why?

The Listening Step

Peter loved Jesus. He wanted to do a job for Jesus. And Jesus had a job for Peter to do.

But Jesus had a question first. "Who do you say that I am?" Jesus asked. That was easy. Peter knew that answer right away. "You are the Christ," Peter said. "The Son of the Living God."

Peter was right. Jesus was the Son of God. "You are Peter," Jesus said. "And upon this Rock I will build my church." Peter's name means "a rock." Jesus was going to start the church. Peter would help Him build it.

Jesus wanted us to be together. He wanted us to worship Him. He wanted to help people learn about Jesus. So Jesus started the church. When we go to church we are doing what Jesus wanted. It is Jesus' church.

The Talking Step

Do you like going to church?

Why?

What does the church mean to you?

✋ The Praying Step

Thank You for my church. Thank you for the pastors and teachers who help me learn about You. Thank You for a free country where we can choose our church.

> So I will call you Peter, which means "a rock." On this rock I will build my church, and death itself will not have any power over it.
>
> —*Matthew 16:18*

The World's Largest Church

Matthew 16:13–20; Acts 2:37–47

 **The Thinking Step**

What is the largest church you have ever attended?

What would a church be like if every Christian in the world attended it?

The Listening Step

Peter was special to Jesus. Jesus called Peter the rock. Jesus had a job for Peter. He said He would use the rock to build His church. Peter was to help Jesus build the church.

Soon Peter had his chance. He told many people about Jesus. Many of them believed in Jesus. They joined the church.

The church was new then. People were joining the church. Everyone who believes in Jesus is part of the church. The church is made up of all believers. It is God's family.

If we believe in Jesus, we are part of the church.

The Talking Step

Ask your mom and dad how many churches they have belonged to. Ask your grandma and grandpa the same question.

How many churches do you think there will be in heaven?

130

 **The Praying Step**

Thank You for my church. Thank You for the teachers and pastors. They help us worship You and learn more about You. It is good to worship You with people who love You as I do.

> But God's Spirit baptized each of us and made us part of the body of Christ.
>
> —*1 Corinthians 12:13*

We Are the Church

1 Corinthians 12:12–31; Ephesians 4:11–16

 **The Thinking Step**

Are you or have you ever been on a team?

Who makes up the team?

If one player left your team, would you still have a team?

The Listening Step

Church means different things. It sometimes means a building. And other times *church* means a program we attend. Paul wrote a letter to the Ephesians. He wanted them to know about the church.

Paul told them. To Paul the church is the people. The church is like our body. Every person in the church is a part of the body. The church body is made of people.

We are the church. Each of us is a special part of the church. We and all our friends are the church.

The Talking Step

What would happen to the church if everyone stopped coming?

How would people act if they knew that they were an important part of the church?

What are things you should do as an important part of the church?

132

The Praying Step

Even though I am young I am important to the church. Help me to know what I can do in the church. Thank You that I can be part of the church team.

Together you are the body of Christ. Each one of you is part of his body.

—1 Corinthians 12:27

The Lord's Supper

Luke 22:1–23

The Thinking Step

Do you know someone who has moved away?
Is there a special way you remember them? What is it?

The Listening Step

Jesus wanted the disciples to remember Him. He wanted to be sure that the people who love Him will always know what He did for us.

So the night before Jesus died He had a special meal. This meal is often called the Last Supper. It was the last meal Jesus ate with the disciples before He died. It was a meal they would remember for a long time.

At the end of the meal Jesus broke a piece of bread. He gave each of the disciples a piece to eat. "This is My body which is given to you." Then Jesus gave them each a drink. "This is My blood which is given for you. Keep doing this to remember Me," Jesus told them.

When we have the Lord's Supper in our church, we should think about Jesus. We should think how He gave His life for us.

The Talking Step

Have you taken part in Communion in your church?
How do they do Communion in your church?
What does Communion mean? Ask your mom or dad to explain it to you.

134

🖐 The Praying Step

Thank You for Communion. It is good that we have a time to remind us of all
You have done for us. It makes me love You more.

> The Lord meant that when you eat this bread and drink from this cup,
> you tell about his death until he comes.
>
> —*1 Corinthians 11:26*

Be Ready for Jesus' Coming

Matthew 24:45–51

The Thinking Step

What is the longest you have had to wait for someone?
What did you do when you were waiting?

The Listening Step

Jesus wanted us to be ready when He returns. So He told the disciples a story about a slave. A slave is someone who works without getting paid. He does what he is told.

One day the master was going away. He told the slave to take care of his family. Then the master returned. He found the slave working hard.

Another master told his slave to take care of his family while he was away. The slave thought the master would be gone a long time. So the slave did not think he had to work hard. But his master came home early.

We do not know when Jesus will return for us. So we need to be ready. We should be looking for His return. And we should be doing what Jesus wants us to do.

The Talking Step

What would Jesus want us to be doing when He returns?
Next time you do something, ask yourself this question: "What would happen if Jesus came back right now?"

 **The Praying Step**

One thing I can be doing for You is telling my friends about You. Give me chances to do that. I know it may be hard sometimes. Help me to always be ready for You to return.

Always be ready! You don't know when the Son of Man will come.

—*Matthew 24:44*

God Will Separate the Good and the Bad

Matthew 25:31–46

The Thinking Step

Have you ever tried to sort your toys?
Do you throw some toys away?
How do you decide which toys to keep?

The Listening Step

One day Jesus will be king. He will return to begin His kingdom on earth. Then He will have special things to do.

He will be like a shepherd. Jesus told the disciples. A shepherd sorts the animals. He puts the sheep on one side. And he puts the goats on the other.

That is what Jesus will do. He will separate everyone. Those of us who believe in Jesus as our Savior will be on one side. Those who did not trust in Jesus as Savior will be on the other side.

The Talking Step

On which side will you be? Why?
Have you asked Jesus to be your Savior?

The Praying Step

Thank You that everything You do is done in love. Thank You for giving us each the chance to choose to trust You as Savior. Help me to tell my friends about You.

Come and receive the kingdom that was prepared for you before the world was created.

—*Matthew 25:34*

God's Home Is Our Home

John 14:15–26; 1 Corinthians 6:12–20

The Thinking Step

Have you ever had someone stay in your house?

Have you ever had someone important stay in your house?

Did this person sleep in your bedroom?

How did your family get the house ready for this person? Why?

The Listening Step

The Christians who lived in Corinth were special. They lived in a big city. It was an important city. They could do many things. But they did not always do the right thing. They did not take care of their bodies very well.

So Paul wrote them a letter. He tried to help them. "Don't you know that your body is where God lives?" Paul asked them. The Holy Spirit lives in our bodies when we are Christians. They had forgotten. He is always inside us. Their bodies had to be a good home for the Holy Spirit.

We must think about this, too. God's home is our body. His home is our home.

The Talking Step

Is your body a good home for the Holy Spirit? Why? Why not?

How could you make your body a better home?

🤚 The Praying Step

My body would be a better home for You if it were cleaner. Forgive my bad thoughts and actions, the times that I don't show love. Help me to keep clean for You.

> Surely you know that your body is a temple where the Holy Spirit lives. The Spirit is in you and is a gift from God. You are no longer your own.
> —*1 Corinthians 6:19*

Heaven Is Our Home

John 14:1–14

The Thinking Step

Where is your home?

Have you ever stayed somewhere else for a summer or other vacation?
Where is your home then?

The Listening Step

Jesus was saying goodbye. His disciples were sad. They would miss Jesus. They did not want Jesus to leave.

But Jesus had good news. "Don't worry," Jesus told His disciples. "There are many rooms in God's house. I am going to prepare a place for you."

The disciples knew this was not a final goodbye. They would see Jesus again. One day they would be with Him forever. Jesus would make a home for them. It would be their heavenly home. They looked forward to that.

The Talking Step

How do you think the disciples felt knowing Jesus would have a home ready for them in heaven?

How did it change the things they did on earth?

How should knowing Jesus has a heavenly home ready for us change the way we live our lives?

✋ The Praying Step

It is so exciting to know You are getting my place in heaven ready! I will love being with You and Your family forever. Thank You, Jesus.

There are many rooms in my Father's house. I wouldn't tell you this, unless it was true. I am going there to prepare a place for each of you.
—*John 14:2*

Here Comes the Judge

Revelation 20:11–15

The Thinking Step

Have you ever been in a courtroom? Have you ever seen a courtroom on television?

What happens?

The Listening Step

John was a special disciple of Jesus. They were close friends. John even wrote a book about Jesus. It is in the Bible. It is called the Gospel of John.

One day God told John what was going to happen. John wrote what God told him. One day Jesus will return, John wrote. He will judge everyone in the world. Jesus will have a big book. This book is called the Book of Life.

Jesus will call the first person up to see Him. Then He will look to see if the person's name is in the Book of Life. If it is not, he will be punished. But if his name is in the Book of Life, he will join the others with Jesus in heaven.

The Book of Life lists everyone's name who has trusted in Jesus as Savior. Our names are in that Book!

The Talking Step

Is your name in the Book of Life? Why? Why not?

Are you looking forward to that day? Why? Why not?

144

 **The Praying Step**

Thank You that my name is in Your Book of Life. I want my friends and family to be with us in heaven. Please help me see times when I can talk to them about You.

> We die only once, and then we are judged.
> —*Hebrews 9:27*

Jesus Has a Surprise

Matthew 24—25

The Thinking Step

Do you like surprises?

Do you like to know *when* the surprise will happen?

How would you feel if you knew what the surprise was but did not know when it would happen?

The Listening Step

Jesus gave the disciples some good news. He also gave them bad news. The bad news was that He was leaving. The good news was that He would return for them.

Jesus told them what would happen in the future. Jesus even told them clues. This way they would know that He was coming soon. But Jesus did not tell them when He would return. That was a surprise!

"It will be like a robber in the middle of the night," Jesus said. No one will know when He is coming. And everybody will be surprised. For Jesus' friends, it will be a surprise worth the wait.

The Talking Step

Why did Jesus not tell us when He will return?

What does Jesus want us to do while we wait?

The Praying Step

When You come back for us, it will be a good surprise for those of us who love You. But, I want everyone to know You. I pray that my friends will come to know You soon, too.

You surely know that the Lord's return will be as a thief coming at night.

—*1 Thessalonians 5:2*

Jesus's Return Is Good News

1 Thessalonians 4:13–18

The Thinking Step

Have you ever had to wait for your mom or dad or best friend to come home?

The Listening Step

Paul had some good friends. He was worried about them. They were getting discouraged. Their neighbors did not like them because they were Christians. They were getting scared.

Paul wanted his friends to know they were doing the right thing. Following Jesus was the right thing to do. So Paul wrote them a letter. "Someday," said Paul, "Jesus will come down from heaven. There will be a shout and the sound of a trumpet. And we will all meet the Lord in the air."

Paul wanted his friends to know that Jesus would come for them. They did not need to worry. He knew that Jesus' return would make them happy.

The Talking Step

Does the return of Jesus make you happy? Why? Why not?

Do you ever get discouraged?

The next time you get discouraged, think about meeting Jesus in the air when He returns for you.

 ## The Praying Step

Sometimes I get discouraged and sad. Sometimes it is hard to think of happy things. Help me to remember the good news—that You are coming to take me to heaven.

We are filled with hope, as we wait for the glorious return of our great God and Savior Jesus Christ.

—Titus 2:13

Jesus Will Bring Us to Heaven

John 14:1–14; Acts 1:1–11; 1 Thessalonians 4:13–18

The Thinking Step

Have you ever waited for someone to pick you up and take you somewhere special?

How did you feel?

The Listening Step

Jesus had just said goodbye to the disciples. But He would be back. The angel said so.

Jesus had told the disciples the same thing. They would remember this. "I will come again," Jesus had said, "and receive you to Myself." Jesus would come again. He would come and get the disciples.

Paul reminded Christians about this. "The trumpet will sound. The Lord will come down. We will meet the Lord in the air."

Jesus will come again. And He will take us to be with Him. He will bring us to Heaven.

The Talking Step

How do you feel about Jesus coming to get us? Why?

Why do you think Jesus is doing this?

What should we be doing while we wait?

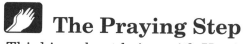 ## The Praying Step

Thinking about being with You in heaven makes me happy. Thank You for dying for my sins and for coming back to get me. Help me to be ready for Your return.

> After I have done this, I will come back and take you with me. Then we will be together.
>
> *—John 14:3*

Jesus Will Come Again

Acts 1:9–11

 ## The Thinking Step

Name a time a close friend or relative left on a long trip.
>Did you miss them?
>Did you know when they would return?
>How did you feel waiting for them to return?

 ## The Listening Step

The disciples were looking up in the sky. Jesus had been taken up into heaven. They were all alone. They did not know what to do. They had been with Jesus for a long time. Now He was gone.

Then they heard a voice. "Why are you standing there looking up into the sky?" the voice said. The disciples all turned around at once. It was an angel! "This same Jesus," the angel said, "will return again the same way He left."

Then they remembered. Jesus said He would go and prepare a place for us. Then He will return for us. They knew it was true.

Jesus will come again. Our job is to tell others about Him until He returns.

 ## The Talking Step

What would Jesus want you to be doing when He returns?
>What would Jesus want you not to be doing?
>What is the best way to wait for Jesus to return?

🤲 The Praying Step

I should be telling my friends and family about You, because You will be coming back very soon. Give me the courage to talk to others about Your love.

Jesus has been taken to heaven. But he will come back in the same way that you have seen him go.

—*Acts 1:11*

The Dead Are Not Dead

1 Thessalonians 4:13–18

The Thinking Step

Have any of the members of your family died?

How did you feel? Why?

Do you think you will see them again?

The Listening Step

The Thessalonians were sad. Many people had died. Some people had lost members of their families. Others had lost good friends. But they were all sad.

Paul wrote them a letter. "Don't be sad," Paul wrote. "When Jesus comes, the first ones to see Him will be those who have died. Then we will all be together with our family and friends and with the Lord."

They felt better now. They would see their friends again. And, best of all, they would be with Jesus.

The Talking Step

Whom are you looking forward to seeing when Jesus returns?

Who might not want Jesus to return?

What can we do to be ready for Jesus?

 **The Praying Step**

I am eager to see my loved ones who have died. It will be great to be with them again when You come back. Thank You for the promise that we will all be together again, if we belong to You.

> With a loud command and with the shout of the chief angel and a blast of God's trumpet, the Lord will return from heaven. Then those who had faith in Christ before they died will be raised to life.
>
> —*1 Thessalonians 4:16*

Waiting for Our Reward

John 15:18—16:6

 The Thinking Step

Have you ever received a reward? What did you do? What reward did you receive?

Did you have to wait for your reward?

The Listening Step

Many people did not believe Jesus. He made many others mad. People did not treat Jesus well. He knew they would treat His helpers badly, too. He warned them.

Soon the disciples knew what Jesus meant. People made fun of them. Some were arrested for talking about Jesus. Some were even killed.

But Jesus told them to keep on going. Keep telling people about Him. If they did, God would reward them. "Your Father who sees in secret," Jesus said, "will reward you openly."

God will reward us for what we do.

The Talking Step

For what would God reward you?

What could you do today for which God would reward you?

✋ The Praying Step

I want You to be happy with me and with what I do for You. Help me to live so that others can see Jesus in me. Thank You for the reward of Your love and eternal life with You.

> The Son of Man will soon come in the glory of His Father and with His angels to reward all people for what they have done.
>
> —*Matthew 16:27*

We Will Be in Heaven with Jesus

John 14:1–14

 The Thinking Step

What do you think heaven will be like?
> Will you like living there?
> Why? Why not?

The Listening Step

Children enjoyed being with Jesus. They liked to play with Him. They followed Jesus as He moved around. Many people followed Him. People liked being with Him. Jesus was very popular.

We can talk with Jesus, too. That is why people pray. It is why they read the Bible. They want to spend time with Jesus. Someday we will see Jesus in person. Then we will be with Him forever.

Jesus said we would be with Him. It will be in heaven. It will be special. Jesus will be there. And we will be with Him, too.

The Talking Step

Are you ready to meet Jesus?
> What will it be like to be with Him all the time?
> What could you do now to be ready for that?

158

 **The Praying Step**

I think heaven is going to be a wonderful place. Thank You that I can be in heaven with You because You sent Jesus to die for my sins. That must have been hard.

> Next, all of us who are still alive will be taken up into the clouds together with them to meet the Lord in the sky. From that time on we will be with the Lord forever.
>
> *—1 Thessalonians 4:17*